DESERT QUARTET

DESERT QUARTET

TERRY TEMPEST WILLIAMS

WITH DRAWINGS AND PAINTINGS BY

MARY FRANK

PANTHEON BOOKS   NEW YORK

The author would like to acknowledge Devon Jersild and David Huddle of the *New England Review*, where "Elements of Love" originally appeared in slightly different form. Gratitude must also be expressed to the Lannan Foundation for their exceptional faith and support in this work.

LIBRARY OF CONGRESS CATALOGING-IN-PUBLICATION DATA

Williams, Terry Tempest
    Desert Quartet/Terry Tempest Williams; illustrations by Mary Frank
    i. cm.
    ISBN 0-679-43999-4
    1. Natural history—Utah. 2. Human ecology. 3. Deserts-Psychological aspects. 4. Williams, Terry Tempest. I. Title.
QH105.U8W54 1995
508.315'4--dc20
                                      95-6091
                                          CIP

Manufactured in the United States of America
First Edition
9 8 7 6 5 4 3 2 1

For Brooke

For the Duration

EARTH

I

Earth. Rock. Desert. I am walking barefoot on sandstone, flesh responding to flesh. It is hot, so hot the rock threatens to burn through the calloused soles of my feet. I must quicken my pace, paying attention to where I step.

For as far as I can see, the canyon country of

southern Utah extends in all directions. No compass can orient me here, only a pledge to love and walk the terrifying distances before me. What I fear and desire most in this world is passion. I fear it because it promises to be spontaneous, out of my control, unnamed, beyond my reasonable self. I desire it because passion has color, like the landscape before me. It is not pale. It is not neutral. It reveals the backside of the heart.

I climb the slickrock on all fours, my hands and feet throbbing with the heat. It feels good to sweat, to be engaged, to inhabit my animal body.

My destination is Druid Arch (by way of the Joint Trail and Chesler Park), located in the southeastern corner of Canyonlands known as the Needles. I have no map, only cairns to guide me, the hand-stacked piles of rocks that say, "Trust me, turn here, I know the way —"

Many resist cairns in the desert, kick them down, believing each traveler should walk on their own authority. It is also true, some cairns have been designed to fool people, to trick them off the trail so they will become lost forever, a quick lesson in self-reliance, to never believe in the stories of

others. But I believe our desire to share is more po-
tent and trustworthy than our desire to be alone.
And so I do not anticipate these markers will lie. To
walk in this country is always an act of faith.

The cairns I have followed have not secured
my own path to intimacy as much as they have given
me the courage to proceed—one foot in front of
the other in a landscape mysterious, unpredictable,
and vast. Nobody really knows the way, that is the
myth of convention.

Cedar Mesa formations of sandstone envelop
me. These pastel cliffs could convince you that you

are a hostage with no way out. But the various shales, softer in character, create the slopes and benches to climb out of one canyon into the heart of another.

Once I enter the Joint Trail, it is as though I am walking through the inside of an animal. It is dark, cool, and narrow with sheer sandstone walls on either side of me. I look up, a slit of sky above. Light is deceptive here. The palms of my hands search for a pulse in the rocks. I continue walking. In some places my hips can barely fit through. I turn sideways, my chest and back in a vise of geologic time.

9

I stop. The silence that lives in these sacred hallways presses against me. I relax. I surrender. I close my eyes. The arousal of my breath rises in me like music, like love, as the possessive muscles between my legs tighten and release. I come to the rock in a moment of stillness, giving and receiving, where there is no partition between my body and the body of Earth.

* * *

There are always logical explanations for the loss of one's mind in the desert. The parallel and intersecting maze I have been traveling through is tortured

rock pulled apart by internal tensions and stresses that form fractures in Earth. These fractures become susceptible to erosion, creating deep slots between fins of sandstone.

Through the weathering of our spirit, the erosion of our soul, we are vulnerable. Isn't that what passion is—bodies broken open through change? We are acted upon. We invite and accept the life of another to take root inside. The succession of the canyons is like our own. A maidenhair fern hangs from the slickrock; water drips, drips, drips, until I catch it in my mouth. Drink deeply, the desert sighs.

For the next few miles I simply walk through the pastoral country of Chesler Park, meadows of serenity. This landscape will take care of me. The open expanse of sky makes me realize how necessary it is to live without words, to be satisfied without answers, to simply be in a world where there is no wind, no drama. To find a place of rest and safety, no matter how fleeting it may be, no matter how illusory, is to regain composure and locate bearings. Picking up stones, I find myself adding to the cairns.

Elephant Canyon is composed of limestone

ledges, turquoise and lavender stairs that eventually lead desert pilgrims to Druid Arch. The vegetation is lush as clumps of milkweed, their orange florescence, attract monarchs in migration. Willows, oak, and single-leaf ash provide cover for collared lizards and towhees. Their shuffling in the dry leaf litter reminds me of all I do not see. And the potholes, sinks of water in the sandstone, beckon me down on hands and knees for a closer look. The minutia of mosquito and mayfly larvae, fairy shrimp, tadpoles, and diving beetles is swirling with its own sense of urgency. Perhaps this is the mind of the lover, manic

and driven, the shallow pools of expectation that inevitably dry up.

Why is it for most of us the vision of the erotic comes as a rare event, a shooting star, a flash flood, a moment of exotic proportion and not in a stable condition?

In this tiny body of water in the desert, I detect waves. I think of the ocean, wave after wave breaking on shore in interminable monotony, yet witnessed, one by one, they can hold us in trance for hours.

The afternoon has delivered me to Druid

Arch. Nothing has prepared me for this insistence of being, the pure artistry of shape and form standing quietly, magnificently in the canyons of Utah. Red rock. Blue sky. This arch is structured metamorphosis. Once a finlike tower, it has been perforated by a massive cave-in, responsible now for the keyholes where wind enters and turns. What has been opened, removed, eroded away, is as compelling to me as what remains. Druid Arch—inorganic matter—rock rising from the desert floor as a creation of time, weathered, broken, and beautiful.

I touch the skin of my face. It seems so callow. Moving my fingers over the soft flesh that covers my cheekbones, I wonder what it means to be human and why at this particular moment, rock seems more accessible and yielding than my own species.

WATER

I I

At first I think it is a small leather pouch some-
one has dropped along the trail. I bend down, pick
it up, and only then recognize it for what it is—a
frog, dead and dried. I have a leather thong in my
pack which I take out and thread through the frog's
mouth and out through its throat. The skin is thin,

which makes a quick puncture possible. I then slide the frog to the center of the thong, tie a knot with both ends, and create a necklace, which I wear.

I grew up with frogs. My brothers and cousins hurled them against canyon walls as we hiked the trail to Rainbow Bridge when Lake Powell was rising behind Glen Canyon Dam.

I hated what they did and told them so. But my cries only encouraged them, excited them, until I became the wall they would throw frogs against. I didn't know what to do—stand still and soften their blow by trying to catch each frog in my hands like a cradle, or turn and run, hoping they would miss me altogether. I tried to believe that somehow the frogs would sail through the air in safety, landing perfectly poised on a bed of moss. But, inevitably, the tiny canyon frogs, about the size of a ripe plum, quickly became entombed in the fists of adolescents and would die on impact, hitting my body, the boys' playing field. I would turn and walk down to the creek and wash the splattered remains off of me. I would enter the water, sit down in the current, and release the frog bodies downstream with my tears.

I never forgave.

21

Years later, my impulse to bathe with frogs is still the same. Havasu. It is only an hour or so past dawn. The creek is cold and clear. I take off my skin of clothes and leave them on the bank. I shiver. How long has it been since I have allowed myself to lie on my back and float? The dried frog floats with me. A slight tug around my neck makes me believe it is still alive, swimming in the current. Travertine ter-

races spill over with turquoise water and we are held in place by a liquid hand that cools and calms the desert.

I dissolve. I am water. Only my face is exposed like an apparition over ripples. Playing with water. Do I dare? My legs open. The rushing water turns my body and touches me with a fast finger that does not tire. I receive without apology. Time. Nothing

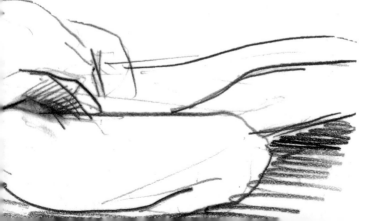

to rush, only to feel. I feel time in me. It is endless pleasure in the current. No control. No thought. Simply, here. My left hand reaches for the frog dangling from my neck, floating above my belly and I hold it between my breasts like a withered heart, beating inside me, inside the river. We are moving downstream. Water. Water music. Blue notes, white notes, my body mixes with the body of water like jazz, the currents like jazz. I too am free to improvise.

I grip stones in shallow water. There is moss behind my fingernails.

I leave the creek and walk up to my clothes. I

am already dry. My skirt and blouse slip on effortlessly. I twist my hair and secure it with a stick. The
frog is still with me. Do I imagine beads of turquoise have replaced the sunken and hollow eyes?

We walk. Canyons within canyons. The sun
threatens to annihilate me. I recall all the oven doors
I have opened to a blast of heat that burned my face.
My eyes narrow. Each turn takes us deeper inside
the Grand Canyon, my frog and I.

We are witnesses to this opening of time, vertical and horizontal at once. Between these crossbars

of geology is a silent sermon on how the world was formed. Seas advanced and retreated. Dunes now stand in stone. Volcanoes erupted and lava has cooled. Garnets shimmer and separate schist from granite. It is sculptured time to be touched, even tasted, our mineral content preserved in the desert.

This is the Rio Colorado.

We are water. We are swept away. Desire begins in wetness. My fingers curl around this little frog. Like me, it was born out of longing, wet, not dry. We can always return to our place of origin. Water. Water music. We are baptized by immersion, nothing less can replenish or restore our capacity to love. It is endless if we believe in water.

We are approaching a cliff. Red monkey flowers bloom. White-throated swifts and violet-green swallows crisscross above. My throat is parched. There is a large pool below. My fear of heights is overcome by my desire to merge. I dive into the water, deeper and deeper, my eyes open, and I see a slender passageway. I wonder if I have enough breath to venture down. I take the risk and swim through the limestone corridor where the water is milky and I can barely focus through the shimmering sediments of sand until it opens into a clear, green room. The frog fetish floats to the surface. I rise too and grab a few breaths held in the top story of this strange cavern. I bump my head on the jagged ceiling. The green room turns red, red, my own blood, my own heart beating, my fingers touch the crown of my head and streak the wall.

Down. I sink back into the current, which carries me out of the underwater maze to the pool. I rise once again, feeling a scream inside me surfacing as I do scream, breathe, tread water, get my bearings. The outside world is green is blue is red is hot, so hot. I swim to a limestone ledge, climb out and lie on my stomach, breathing. The rock is steaming. The frog is under me. Beating. Heart beating. I am dry. I long to be wet. I am bleeding. Back on my knees, I immerse my head in the pool once more to ease the cut and look below. Half in. Half out. Amphibious. I am drawn to both Earth and water. The frog breaks free from the leather thong. I try to grab its body but miss and watch it slowly spiral into the depths.

* * *

Before leaving, I drink from a nearby spring and hold a mouthful—I hear frogs, a chorus of frogs, their voices rising like bubbles from what seems to be the green room. Muddled at first, they become clear. I run back to the edge of the pool and listen—

throwing back my head, I burst into laughter spray-
ing myself with water.

It is rain.

It is frogs.

It is hearts breaking against the bodies of
those we love.

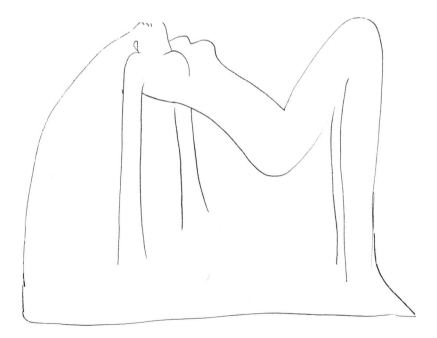

FIRE

III

I strike a match and light the shreds of kin-dling I have cut with my knife. Juniper. I fan the in-cense toward me. The smoke rises, curls, coils around my face. It feels good to be in the desert again. Home—where I can pause, remain silent. There is nothing to explain.

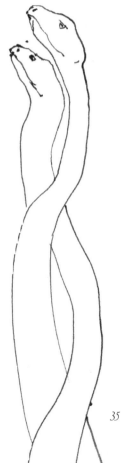

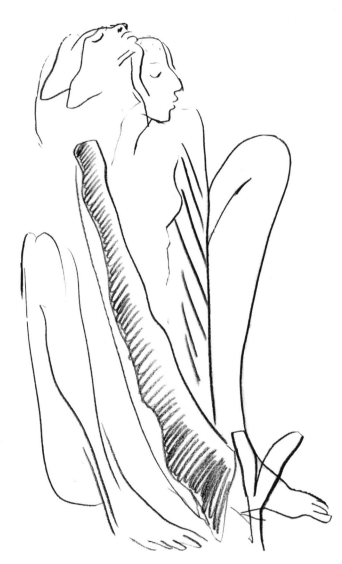

36

I break twigs and lean them against each other in the formation of a teepee. More smoke. On hands and knees in red sand, I blow at its base, blow again, add a handful of dried cottonwood leaves, blow, they ignite, flames engulf the triangle.

I sit back on my haunches, pleased that the fire is growing in the desert, in me, so that I can dream, remember, how it is that I have come to love. It is fate that determines the territory of the heart. I add more sticks, blow, the fire flares in darkness.

The wood opens.

Flames rise, flicker. My eyes blur. I hold every

detail of love in my body, nothing forgotten, put more sticks on the fire. It surges, sputters, and purrs. The fire holds me captive, charismatic flames wave me closer. I add two more sticks like bodies to love. They are consumed instantly. The fire shifts, then settles with new intensity; it shifts again, adjusts. The wood pops like vertebrae. The silver bark of juniper burns black, turns white. A spark breathes.

I crouch down and blow on embers. They flare and quiver. I blow again. They become rubies. I

reach into the coals, believing, and burn my fingers, blister their tips, pull back in pain and bury my hands in the sand. The fire wanes. I cannot bear its absence. I lower my head and blow. The fire ignites. My longing returns. When we want everything to change we call on fire.

I fetch more wood. Bones of pinyon and juniper lie on the desert floor. Even in darkness I see them illumined by the moon. I gather them in my arms. This time they are larger. I must break them over my knee and feed the fire once again. The fire is aroused. The flames reach higher. I stand before them with my arms raised, my hands surrender and come down to caress the heat and mold it into faces I love. Do I dare to feel the white heat of my heart as a prayer? What is smoldering inside me? And how is it that pleasure exists between such beauty and violence? Feed the fire. No. Yes. My fingers touch the blaze of bodies in flames.

The fire explodes. Flames become blue tongues curling around each other. My eyes close. I step forward. My legs open to the heat, the tingling return of heat, inside, outside, shadows dance on the sandstone, my ghostly lover. I allow myself to be ravished. My generosity becomes my humiliation. The hair between my legs is singed. My left hand

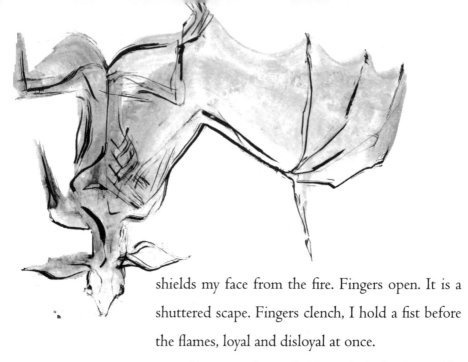

shields my face from the fire. Fingers open. It is a shuttered scape. Fingers clench, I hold a fist before the flames, loyal and disloyal at once.

Above me, free-tailed bats circle the flames like

moths. Moths frighten me. I hate their addiction to light. But bats delight in darkness with their ears wide open. What do they hear that I am missing? Gifted in the location of echoes, they listen twice to all that is spoken in the desert. They are dark angels who register our longings and pinpoint the cries lodged within our throats.

Heat. More heat. My face flushes red. The fire's hands are circling. I sit inches away from something that tomorrow will not exist. The blue-eyed coals I gaze into will disappear. Ashes. Ashes. Death is the natural conclusion of love.

But tonight it remains alive and I know in the shock of my heart that love is as transitory as fire. The warmth I feel, the glow of my body and the force of my own interior heat, is enough to keep me here.

It is our nature to be aroused—not once, but again and again. Where do we find the strength to not be pulled apart by our passions? How do we inhabit the canyons inside a divided heart? One body. Two bodies. Three.

Beyond the junipers and pinyons of this starless night, I face the deep stare of darkness. This

45

wildness cannot be protected or preserved. There is little forgiveness here. Experience is the talisman I hold for courage. It is the desert that persuades me toward love, to step outside and defy custom one more time.

The fire now bears the last testament to trees. I blow into the religious caverns of wood and watch them burn brightly. My breath elucidates each yellow room and I remember the body as sacrament.

I have brought white candles with me. I take them out of my pouch and secure them in the sand. With a small stick I carry a flame from the fire and

light one, and another, and another. They threaten
to flicker and fade. I shelter them with my hands
and watch the way the wax trickles down the side of
each taper. Once away from the flame, it hardens.
My body reflects back the heat. I dip the tip of my

finger into the small basin of heated wax shining at the base of the wick, bring it to my lips and paint them.

I turn toward the flames.

AIR

I V

I hear it coming up through the rocks. It is a geyser of air that draws me farther up the red stone staircase. I look down over my shoulder to the river valley below and almost lose my nerve, but something pulls me higher, takes hold of my spine and stretches me.

I am not alone. Handprints are stamped on the staircase walls. I mime my hands with theirs. The Anasazi have never left.

I kneel at the mouth where the rock lips are open, a column of wind is wafting, rushing up from the center of Earth. I try to shape a voice, to feel its words through the delicacy of my fingers, but it is not to be touched. My hands are pushed back by its force until my mouth is covered.

In the beginning, there were no words.

I am behind the rocks. I strain to see what it is, who it is, try to blow it out like a candle flame to see if a trail of smoke will curl and wrap itself around me, offering clues as to how it moves in the world. But it is not to be seen.

There is nothing to taste.

There is nothing to smell.

I inch back, precarious, and focus on breath. Inhale. Exhale. Inhale. Exhale. The attention of breath in love, two breaths creating a third, mingling and shaping each other like clouds, cumulus clouds

over the desert. On my back, I reclaim the sweet and simple ecstasy of breathing. The wind becomes a wail, a proper lament for all that is hidden. Inhale. Exhale. This is the dreamtime of the desert, the beginning of poetry.

My body softens as I make my wish to follow my breath. It settles on the backs of swallowtails. We are carried effortlessly through the labyrinth of these labial canyons.

Breath becomes a lizard, hands splayed on red rock walls. Up and down. Up and down. A raven lands, black wings are extended like arms.

The Animals know.

The Anasazi know.

It is audible.

I lean forward and listen. Breath. With my hands on the rocks, I place my mouth over the opening. My belly rises and falls. I move away and listen. I return with my mouth over the opening. Inhale. Exhale. I move away. I listen. I return.

I am dizzy. I am drunk with pleasure. There is no need to speak.

Listen.

Below us.

Above us.

Inside us.

Come.

This is all there is.

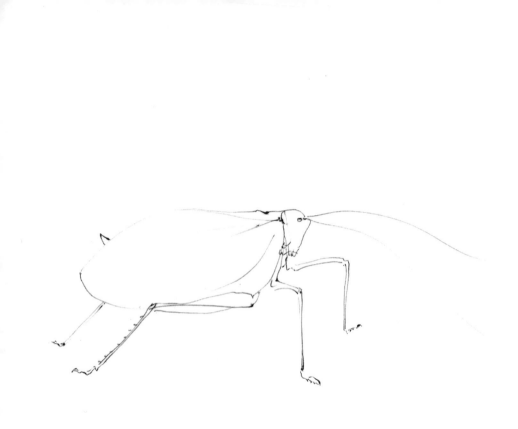

Acknowledgments

We would like to acknowledge the friendship of Linda Asher, who brought us together; the music of David Darling and Mickey Houlihan, *Eight String Religion,* inspired by the Colorado Plateau; the Southern Utah Wilderness Alliance, who remain vigilant in the preservation of these sacred lands; Dan Frank, our editor;

Fearn Cutler, who designed this book; Carl Brandt, our mediator; and, of course, Brooke Williams and Leo Treitler, who understand the body as landscape.

About the Authors

Terry Tempest Williams is naturalist-in-residence at the Utah Museum of Natural History. Her books include *Pieces of White Shell, Coyote's Canyon, Refuge,* and *An Unspoken Hunger.* She is the recipient of a Lannan Fellowship in creative nonfiction.

Mary Frank's work has been widely exhibited and is held in many public collections, including the Metropolitan Museum of Art, the Art Institute of Chicago, and the Museum of Fine Arts in Boston. She is an environmental activist and collaborated with Peter Matthiessen on *Shadows of Africa.* She was the subject of a comprehensive monograph by Hayden Herrera, published in 1990. Mary Frank is represented by the Midtown Payson Gallery in New York City.

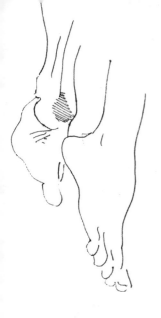

A Note on the Type

This book was set in Centaur, designed by Bruce Rogers (1870-1957) for the exclusive use of The Metropolitan Museum of Art in New York. Rogers was influenced by the elegant Roman typefaces of the fifteenth-century printer Nicolas Jensen and the work of his contemporary William Morris of the Kelmscott Press in England. Centaur is considered by many to be one of the finest types produced in this century, for its beautiful calligraphic quality and its exceptional readability.

Printed and bound by Quebecor Printing/Kingsport, Tenn.
Designed and typeset by Fearn Cutler de Vicq de Cumptich